LEARN ABOUT VALUES

RESPECT

by Cynthia A. Klingel

The Child's World®

Published in the United States of America by The Child's World®
1980 Lookout Drive • Mankato, MN 56003-1705 • 800-599-READ • www.childsworld.com

The Child's World®: Mary Berendes, Publishing Director; Katherine Stevenson, Editor
The Design Lab: Kathy Petelinsek, Art Director; Julia Goozen, Design and Page Production

Photo Credits: © John Henley/Corbis: 7; © Randy Faris/Corbis: cover; © Thinkstock/Corbis: 19;
All other photos © David M. Budd Photography

Library of Congress Cataloging-in-Publication Data
Klingel, Cynthia Fitterer.
  Respect / by Cynthia A. Klingel.
     p. cm. — (Learn about values)
  ISBN 978-1-59296-675-2 ISBN 1-59296-675-6 (library bound: alk. paper)
  1. Respect—Juvenile literature. 2. Values—Juvenile literature. I. Title. II. Series.
  BJ1533.R4K55 2006
  179'.9—dc22   2006000964

CONTENTS

What Is Respect?

When you respect people, you treat them well. You **consider** their needs and feelings. You are careful about what you do and say to them. You are fair to them. You treat them as you would like to be treated.

Showing respect means making sure everyone gets a fair chance.

Respecting Others

You know that good manners are important. You say "please" and "thank you." You talk quietly when you are in a library. You do not yell at people. You do not bother people when they are busy. Using good manners shows respect for the people around you.

You can respect others in a library by reading quietly.

Respect at School

Your teacher asks another student a question. You know the answer! You raise your hand. Your teacher waits for the other student to answer. You show respect by being quiet and **patient**. You let the other student answer.

Waiting your turn shows respect for others.

Respecting Other People's Things

Your sister has a special game. You love to play it! She lets you use it when she is gone. When you are done, you put it away. You are careful not to lose any pieces. You show respect for your sister by being careful with her game.

You can show respect by taking good care of people's things.

Respecting Other People's Needs

Your brother does his homework in the kitchen. He needs quiet time to do a good job. You and a friend feel like playing. You would like to use the kitchen table. But you respect your brother's needs. You play in another room instead.

Paying attention to other people's needs shows respect.

13

Respecting Other People's Homes

You are playing ball in your yard. The ball bounces into your neighbor's garden. Your neighbor loves to work in her garden. She works hard to make her flowers grow. You could stomp through quickly to get your ball. But you step carefully. You respect your neighbor. So you are careful not to harm her garden.

Being careful can be a way of showing respect.

15

Respecting Your Parents

Your parents want you to keep your room clean. They want you to set the table for meals. They have rules you need to follow. You do not always want to do these things. But you show respect for your parents by following their rules.

Following rules shows respect for the people who made them.

Respecting Your Country

You go to a baseball game. Before it begins, the nation's **anthem** is played. You stop talking to your friends. You place your hand over your heart. You look at the flag and sing along. It feels good to show respect for your flag and country. Showing respect for your country is called **patriotism**.

There are lots of ways to show respect for your country.

Showing Respect Helps Everyone

Respecting others makes them feel good. It also makes them think kindly of you. It makes you feel good, too. When you respect others, they will respect you in return. That helps everybody get along better!

Showing respect is a great way to show that you care!

21

glossary

anthem
An anthem is a national song. The anthem of the U.S.A. is "The Star-Spangled Banner."

consider
If you consider something, you think about it carefully.

patient
Being patient means waiting for something without getting upset.

patriotism
Patriotism is a feeling of love and respect for your country.

books

Dylan, Matthew. *Respect.* Austin, TX: Raintree Steck-Vaughn, 2002.

Loewen, Nancy, and Omarr Wesley. *Treat Me Right: Kids Talk about Respect.* Minneapolis, MN: Picture Window Books, 2002.

Meiners, Cheri J., and Meredith Johnson. *Respect and Take Care of Things.* Minneapolis, MN: Free Spirit, 2004.

web sites

Visit our Web page for links about character education and values:
http://www.childsworld.com/links

Note to parents, teachers, and librarians:
We routinely check our Web links to make sure they're safe, active sites—so encourage your readers to check them out!

index

about the author

Cynthia A. Klingel is Director of Curriculum and Instruction for a school district in Minnesota. She enjoys reading, writing, gardening, traveling, and spending time with friends and family.